cocktails

by James Butler and Vicki Liley

TUTTLE PUBLISHING
Tokyo • Rutland, Vermont • Singapore

Published by Tuttle Publishing, an imprint of Periplus
Editions (HK) Ltd., with editorial offices at 364 Innovation
Drive, North Clarendon, Vermont 05759 USA and
61 Tai Seng Avenue, #02-12, Singapore 534167

Hardcover ISBN 13: 978-0-8048-3865-8
        ISBN 10: 0-8048-3865-8
Printed in Malaysia

Distributed by
North America, Latin America and Europe
Tuttle Publishing, 364 Innovation Drive,
North Clarendon, VT 05759-9436 U.S.A.
Tel: 1 (802) 773-8930; Fax: 1 (802) 773-6993
info@tuttlepublishing.com
www.tuttlepublishing.com

Japan
Tuttle Publishing, Yaekari Building, 3rd Floor
5-4-12 Osaki, Shinagawa-ku, Tokyo 141 0032.
Tel: (81) 03 5437-0171; Fax: (81) 03 5437-0755
tuttle-sales@gol.com

Asia Pacific
Berkeley Books Pte Ltd.
61 Tai Seng Avenue, #02-12
Singapore 534167.
Tel: (65) 6280-1330 Fax: (65) 6280-6290
inquiries@periplus.com.sg
www.periplus.com

10 09 08
5 4 3 2

TUTTLE PUBLISHING® is a registered trademark of Tuttle Publishing,
a division of Periplus Editions (HK) Ltd.

Contents

A Touch of Fun and Glamour   6

Glassware   8

Bar Equipment   10

Mixing Techniques   12

Garnishes and Decorations   14

Essential Cocktail Ingredients   15

Classic Cocktails   16

Champagne Cocktails   34

Martinis   40

Blended Cocktails   48

Crushed Cocktails   60

Built Cocktails   68

Shaken and Strained
   Cocktails   80

Nonalcoholic Cocktails   88

Hot Drinks   92

Ingredient Glossary   94

Complete List of Recipes   96

A Touch of Fun and Glamour

The cocktail was born in the United States in the nineteenth century. Exactly who and where remains controversial, but there's no denying that the United States has been almost single-handedly responsible for the drink's popularity and growth.

These days, there are more cocktails than you can count. Virtually any alcoholic liquid and flavoring can be combined and new cocktails are being invented all the time. Most are based on spirits and served chilled or with ice. They can be as simple as a classic martini or as complex as a margarita, where citrus juice and tequila are sipped from a glass rimmed with salt.

The way you mix a cocktail depends on its ingredients, but it's an art easily mastered. Liquids of similar densities can be stirred. Limpid, transparent ingredients call for gentle stirring, as too much agitation can cause the cocktail to turn cloudy. Vigorous agitation is called for, however, when mixing liquids of different densities: spirits and syrups or liqueurs, as in a margarita.

You'll find that a genuine cocktail shaker will come in handy, as it allows you to chill and blend ingredients simultaneously. Ice is added to the shaker, but is prevented by a strainer from entering the glass.

Another useful item is a blender, for preparing cocktails that include solid ingredients. Fruit, for example, can be reduced to a purée, and ice cubes cracked into smaller pieces give a daiquiri its pleasantly granular texture. Some cocktails containing solid ingredients rely for their success on the aromatic flavors of oils being released into the glass. If you're preparing a caipirinha, you'll need to use a muddler (see page 10) or the back of a spoon to crush the cut fruit and extract that unmistakable fresh citrus taste. Mint juleps call for mint leaves and sugar to be ground together to enhance the drink's citrus overtones.

And let's not forget the ice. It's not there simply to cool the drink. Whole ice cubes melt slowly and are best when you want maximum coldness with minimum dilution. Crushed ice introduces its own texture but also melts quickly enough to dilute a strong drink. Whichever kind of ice you use, remember that cubes made with bottled water frozen shortly before using will taste a whole lot better than that chlorinated liquid you get from a tap. Don't ruin good liquor with bad water.

Above all, don't forget that cocktails are meant to be fun. It doesn't matter whether they're classic and sophisticated or modern and innovative. They can be served at an intimate dinner party—before, during or after—or just to unwind after a hard day.

But wherever cocktails are served, they introduce a touch of glamour that you just don't get with other drinks.

RIGHT: Killer Martini
(see page 40 for recipe)

Glassware

Everyone agrees a drink tastes much better when served in a beautiful glass and a cocktail seems to have more importance when it is served in a special glass.

The champagne flute: 8–14 oz (250–430 ml) Elegant and long stemmed, with a narrow rim, the champagne flute is artfully designed to conserve the natural bubbles in Champagne.

The martini and cocktail glass: 6–8 oz (180–250 ml) The martini glass has an open face, a thin stem and a V-shaped bowl. The cocktail glass is similar, but has a slightly rounded bowl. It is not essential to have both glasses.

The highball or collins glass: 8–10 oz (250–300 ml) The highball, or collins glass, can vary greatly in style and size, but is always tall and slim, designed to keep a long drink cold.

The old-fashioned or rocks glass: 6–10 oz (180–300 ml) The old-fashioned, or rocks glass, is short and straight sided. It has a heavy base and is comfortable to hold. Drinks served in these glasses are generally meant to be enjoyed slowly.

Note on measurements: Please note that all alcohol measurements in this book are given in oz and ml. 1–1$1/_2$ oz (30–45 ml) is approximately equivalent to one jigger. $1/_2$ oz (15 ml) is equivalent to one US/UK tablespoon. $2/_3$ oz (20 ml) is equivalent to one Australian tablespoon. All recipes serve 1 unless otherwise stated.

Bar Equipment

Having the correct bar equipment for constructing cocktails will make the experience more fun and enjoyable. Other useful equipment for your cocktail bar includes measuring spoons and cups, a citrus juicer, an ice bucket and ice tongs, and a blender.

Bar spoon: A long, flat-headed spoon with a twisted shaft, used for stirring drinks, pouring layered drinks and muddling or crushing.

Muddler: A wooden pestle used for mixing or crushing ingredients such as sugar cubes and mint. If you don't have one, use a mortar and pestle.

Jigger: A double-headed jigger is best. It holds liquid measures of 1 oz (30 ml) and $1^1/_2$ oz (45 ml).

Strainer: A strainer is used to pour shaken drinks through into the glass. The Hawthorn strainer (pictured) has a spring coiled around its head. The spring fits neatly inside a glass to hold the strainer in place.

Shaker (right): There are two types of shakers. The most common, available in department stores, is the stainless-steel cocktail shaker. This usually consists of three parts: a small lid, the strainer and the receptacle. Before shaking a drink, always make sure that the shaker is assembled correctly. The other type of shaker is called a Boston shaker; it is half stainless steel and half glass.

Mixing Techniques

Shaking: Shaking cocktails can be fun for you and your guests. Fill a shaker with ice cubes before adding your favorite cocktail ingredients. Shake up and down for about 10 seconds, a little longer for cocktails with egg white and/or cream bases. Always make sure you hold the lid while shaking. Remove the lid and strain the contents into the desired glass.

Stirring: This is the best method when you require clarity of the spirits. Martinis, for example, should always be stirred. Use an ice-filled glass, and stir carefully with a bar spoon. Another method is to gently swirl the spirits in an ice-filled cocktail shaker, then strain them into a chilled glass. With both methods, be careful not to chip the ice, thus diluting the drink.

Blending: Ice and the cocktail ingredients are combined in a blender and processed until smooth.

Building: This is the simplest method of making cocktails. The measured cocktail ingredients are added to an ice-filled glass and given, if needed, a quick stir.

Muddling (left): This is a process of pressing and pounding a wooden pestle into fruit, sugar and/or herbs in the base of a heavy old-fashioned or rocks glass. Muddling allows flavors to be released gently.

Garnishes and Decorations

Garnishes for cocktails can be as simple as a citrus twist or a single olive on a toothpick, or fun and colorful for a party atmosphere.

Use a vegetable peeler to shave thin lengthwise slices from a cucumber. Wind into a glass before filling.

Kitschy drink stirrers make simple garnishes for cocktails in old-fashioned and highball glasses.

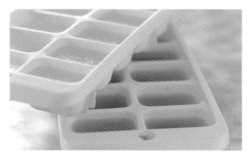

Fill ice cube trays with fruit juice, then freeze and add the flavored ice cubes to your favorite cocktails.

Paper parasols are available in a wide variety of colors and patterns.

Rub a cut lime along the rim of the glass, then upend into a saucer filled with sea salt, pepper or sugar.

Fresh fruits such as berries make tasteful, simple and edible garnishes.

Essential Cocktail Ingredients

Flavored spirits: Any spirit can be flavored with a variety of fruits, herbs and spices, from chili to citrus. Add your chosen flavoring to your favorite spirit, seal and let the mixture stand in a cool, dark place for at least 1 month.

Fruit purée: Place a small amount of the desired fruit and 1 tablespoon of sugar syrup in a food processor or blender, and process until smooth. Use as required in fruit cocktails.

Sugar syrup: Combine 1 cup (200 g) of sugar and 1 cup (250 ml) of water in a small saucepan and bring to a boil over medium heat, stirring until the sugar is dissolved. Remove from the heat and cool. Pour into a bottle, seal and store in the refrigerator.

Syrups: These commercial syrups add complexity and flavor to a drink. Usually nonalcoholic or quite low in alcohol (less than 3 percent), they come in many flavors, including cherry, strawberry, raspberry, coconut, pineapple and ginger.

Classic Cocktails

Classic cocktails are an exclusive club—one with just a few distinguished members but the largest fan club since Elvis. And they're the best way to test a new bar or mixologist. Ask for a classic you know and love, then keep score. Do they use a good, dark rum in Mai Tai? Is the Bellini made with fresh peaches? Is the Sea Breeze bitter, yet thirst-quenching? This is the kind of exam the bar staff will need to pass to get into Cocktail College!

It really shouldn't be too difficult. The following classics have been around for years, most of them for decades and they've stood the tests of time, fashion and fad. Like a good cigar, they're straightforward and have a certain dignity about them. Content to wait in the wings while more exotic, upstart creations have their fifteen minutes of fame, the classics are today more popular than ever.

Like timeless movies or tunes, classic cocktails are conversation starters, historical icons and definitions of good taste that bring with them the memories of special times and places. And you know what they say about the benefits of a classical education, so put your head down and study a few of these before you send out your next invitations, whether the gathering is sophisticated or casual. There's a lot to be said for the keep-it-simple formula when it comes to party drinks, and these smooth-talkers know exactly how to say "welcome."

Bloody Mary

Ice cubes
2 oz (60 ml) vodka
$^1/_2$ oz (15 ml) fresh lemon juice
6 oz (180 ml) tomato juice
Dash of Tabasco sauce
2 dashes Worcestershire sauce
1 teaspoon horseradish sauce
Ground white pepper
Celery stick and pinch of ground
  black pepper, to garnish

Half fill a cocktail shaker with some ice cubes. Add the vodka, lemon juice, tomato juice and sauces. Shake and strain the mixture into a white pepper-rimmed glass. Garnish with a celery stick and pinch of ground black pepper.

Long Island Iced Tea

Ice cubes
1 oz (30 ml) vodka
1 oz (30 ml) gin
1 oz (30 ml) light rum
1 oz (30 ml) tequila
1 oz (30 ml) fresh lemon juice
Coca-Cola, chilled

Fill a highball glass with some ice cubes. Add the vodka, gin, rum, tequila and lemon juice. Top with some chilled Coca-Cola and stir.

Singapore Sling

Ice cubes
1 oz (30 ml) gin
1 oz (30 ml) fresh lemon juice
Dash of Cointreau
Dash of Bénédictine
Dash of pineapple juice
Dash of Cherry Heering liqueur
Orchid blossom, to garnish

Fill a highball glass with ͏ lemon juice, Cointreau, ͏ juice, and stir. Pour the ͏ of the drink and garnish ͏

OPPOSITE: Long Island Iced Tea
RIGHT: Singapore Sling

Moscow Mule

Ice cubes
2 lime wedges
2 oz (60 ml) vodka
1/2 oz (15 ml) fresh lime juice
Ginger beer, chilled
Fresh pineapple leaves, to garnish

Fill a highball glass with some ice cubes and add the lime wedges. Add the vodka and lime juice, top with the ginger beer and stir. Garnish with pineapple leaves.

Manhattan

3 oz (90 ml) Canadian whiskey
1/2 oz (15 ml) Dry Vermouth
1/2 oz (15 ml) Sweet Vermouth
Dash of Angostura bitters
Stemmed cherry or lemon twist,
   to garnish

Pour all the ingredients into a mixing glass, stir and strain into a small chilled martini glass. Garnish with a stemmed cherry.

Note: For the **Dry** version, mix the ingredients as instructed but without the Sweet Vermouth, then garnish with a lemon twist. For the **Sweet** version, omit the Dry Vermouth and garnish with a stemmed cherry.

James Bond

1 sugar cube
Angostura bitters, for soaking
1 oz (30 ml) vodka
Champagne, chilled

Soak the sugar cube in the Angostura bitters, then place it in a champagne saucer or flute. Pour the vodka over the sugar cube and top with the chilled Champagne.

OPPOSITE: Moscow Mule,
RIGHT: James Bond

Bellini

1 peach wedge
$1/_2$ fresh ripe peach, peeled and
   pitted
$1/_2$ oz (15 ml) peach liqueur
Champagne, chilled

Place the peach wedge in a champagne flute. Process the peach half in a blender and pour the purée into the glass. Add the peach liqueur, top with some chilled Champagne and stir gently.

Gimlet

Ice cubes
2 oz (60 ml) gin
Lime cordial or fresh lime juice
1 lime twist, to garnish

Combine all the ingredients (except the lime twist) in a mixing glass, stir and strain into a chilled martini glass. Garnish with the lime twist.

Kir Royale

$1/_4$ oz ($7^1/_2$ ml) crème de cassis
Champagne, chilled

Pour the crème de cassis into a champagne flute, then top with the chilled Champagne.

LEFT: Bellini
RIGHT: Kir Royale

Margarita

Ice cubes
2 oz (60 ml) tequila
1 oz (30 ml) Cointreau
1 oz (30 ml) fresh lemon juice
1 oz (30 ml) fresh lime juice
Dash of lightly beaten egg white
Coarse salt

Fill a cocktail shaker with some ice cubes. Add the tequila, Cointreau, lemon juice, lime juice and egg white, then shake and strain into a salt-rimmed martini glass.

Pina Colada

Ice cubes
1$^{1}/_{2}$ oz (45 ml) rum
2 oz (60 ml) pineapple juice
$^{1}/_{4}$ cup (60 ml) coconut cream
2 pineapple leaves or 1 sprig of
  mint, to garnish

Combine all the ingredients, except the garnish, in a shaker and mix. Serve over ice, or blend with some crushed ice, garnished with the pineapple leaves or mint.

Caipirinha

1 lime, cut into eighths
3 brown sugar cubes
Ice cubes
2 oz (60 ml) cachaça

Place the lime and sugar cubes in an old-fashioned glass. Muddle until the juice is extracted and the sugar is crushed. Fill the glass with some ice cubes and top with the cachaça, and stir.

OPPOSITE: Margarita
RIGHT: Caipirinha

Sea Breeze

Ice cubes
2 lime wedges
2 oz (60 ml) vodka
Cranberry juice, chilled
Grapefruit juice, chilled
1 lime slice, to garnish

Fill a highball or collins glass with some ice cubes and squeeze the lime wedges over the ice. Pour in the vodka and fill the glass three-quarters full with the cranberry juice. Top with the grapefruit juice, stir and garnish with the lime slice.

Grasshopper

Ice cubes
1 oz (30 ml) green crème de menthe
1 oz (30 ml) white crème de cacao
2 tablespoons heavy cream
Sugar

Fill a cocktail shaker with some ice cubes. Add the crème de menthe, crème de cacao and cream, then shake and strain into a sugar-rimmed martini glass.

LEFT: Sea Breeze
RIGHT: Grasshopper

Cosmopolitan

Ice cubes
2 oz (60 ml) Absolut Citron vodka
1 oz (30 ml) Cointreau
1 oz (30 ml) fresh lime juice
1 oz (30 ml) cranberry juice
Dash of lightly beaten egg white
Fresh pineapple leaves, to garnish

Fill a cocktail shaker with some ice cubes. Add the vodka, Cointreau, lime juice, cranberry juice and egg white, then shake and strain the mixture into a large martini glass. Garnish with the pineapple leaves.

Mint Julep

5–6 fresh mint leaves
2 sugar cubes
Ice cubes
3 oz (90 ml) bourbon

Place the mint and sugar in an old-fashioned glass and muddle until the juice is extracted and the sugar is crushed. Fill the glass with some ice cubes, then pour the bourbon over and stir.

Tom Collins

Ice cubes
1 oz (30 ml) fresh lemon juice
1 oz (30 ml) gin
Dash of sugar syrup
Soda water, chilled
1 lemon slice, to garnish

Fill a highball glass with some ice cubes and add the lemon juice, gin and sugar syrup. Top with some chilled soda water and stir, then garnish with lemon slice.

Rob Roy

Ice cubes
1 1/2 oz (45 ml) scotch
3/4 oz (23 ml) Sweet Vermouth
1 lemon twist, to garnish

Combine all the ingredients (except the lemon twist) in a mixing glass, then stir and strain into a chilled martini glass. Garnish with the lemon twist.

RIGHT: Cosmopolitan

Daiquiri

Ice cubes
2 oz (60 ml) Bacardi white rum
2 oz (60 ml) fresh lime juice
Dash of sugar syrup
1 lime wedge, to garnish

Fill a cocktail shaker with some ice cubes and add the rum, lime juice and sugar syrup. Shake and strain the mixture into a chilled cocktail or large martini glass, and garnish with the lime wedge.

Mojito

5 fresh mint leaves
2 sugar cubes
2 lime wedges
Ice cubes
2 oz (60 ml) Bacardi white rum
Soda water, chilled

Place the mint leaves and sugar cubes in an old-fashioned glass and muddle until the sugar is crushed. Add the lime wedges and muddle again until the juice is extracted. Fill the glass with some ice cubes and pour the rum over. Top with the chilled soda water and stir.

LEFT: Daiquiri
RIGHT: Mojito

Mai Tai

1 long strip orange zest
Ice cubes
1^1/$_2$ oz (45 ml) light rum
^{1}/$_3$ oz (10 ml) curaçao
^{1}/$_3$ oz (10 ml) fresh lime juice
^{1}/$_2$ oz (15 ml) pineapple juice
Dash of Angostura bitters
2 dashes orgeat syrup
Fresh mint leaves and 1 orange
  wedge, to garnish

Wind the strip of orange zest into a highball glass. Fill the glass and a cocktail shaker with some ice cubes. Add the rum, curaçao, juices, bitters and orgeat syrup to the shaker, then shake and strain the mixture into the ice-filled glass. Garnish with the mint leaves and orange wedge.

Brandy Alexander

Ice cubes
2 oz (60 ml) brandy
^{1}/$_2$ oz (15 ml) crème de cacao
1 tablespoon half-and-half cream
  (half milk, half cream)
Ground nutmeg, for dusting

Fill a cocktail shaker with some ice cubes and add the brandy, crème de cacao and cream. Shake and pour the mixture into a cocktail glass, then dust with the ground nutmeg.

OPPOSITE: Mai Tai
RIGHT: Brandy Alexander

Champagne Cocktails

Why is it that Champagne (with or without the uppercase "C" reserved for the "real McCoy" from the Champagne region of northeast France) always makes you feel happy, even bringing out a sense of humor in the normally dour duke? Served in a cocktail at a party or as a pre-dinner drink, this nose-tingling fizz imparts a fabulous sense of fun and enjoyment, and an expectation of good times ahead.

There's the school of thought that claims Champagne is best enjoyed chilled and on its own. But a fine-tasting Champagne can actually be improved by mixing it with ingredients that enhance its taste. The results can be absolutely stunning!

Well-known classic Champagne cocktails, such as James Bond (page 20), Bellini and Kir Royale (page 23), happily marry chilled Champagne with just one other simple flavoring.

If you can't afford French Champagne, substitute a good sparkling wine from California. These New World "champagnes" are made from the same grapes (chardonnay, pinot noir or pinot blanc) as their French cousins, frequently by U.S. subsidiaries of the French parent. There are also endless varieties of German sekt or Italian spumante that work just as well.

What are the rules for Champagne cocktail success?

1. Keep it simple.
2. Always use chilled Champagne.
3. Always add the Champagne to the cocktail last (that way you'll keep the bubbles bubbling).
4. Don't expect the taste of a cheap Champagne to improve when used in a cocktail.

French 75

Ice cubes
$1/_2$ oz (15 ml) gin
$1/_2$ oz (15 ml) fresh lemon juice
Dash of sugar syrup
Champagne, chilled

Fill a highball glass with some ice cubes and add the gin, lemon juice and sugar syrup. Top with the Champagne and stir.

Alasia

2 teaspoons raspberry purée
$1/2$ oz (15 ml) crème de framboise
Champagne, chilled
3 fresh raspberries, to garnish

Pour the raspberry purée and crème de framboise into a champagne flute, and top with the chilled Champagne. Garnish with the raspberries.

Peach Bubbles

Ice cubes
$1/3$ oz (10 ml) peach schnapps
Dash of peach nectar
Ruby red grapefruit juice
Champagne, chilled
1 ruby red grapefruit wedge,
  to garnish

Fill a highball glass with some ice cubes. Pour the peach schnapps and nectar over the ice and half fill the glass with the grapefruit juice. Top with the chilled Champagne and garnish with the grapefruit wedge.

RIGHT: Alasia,
LEFT: Peach Bubbles

Croatian Cherry

$1/_2$ oz (15 ml) sour cherry syrup
$1/_2$ oz (15 ml) sloe gin
Champagne, chilled
Cherries, to garnish

Pour the syrup and sloe gin into a champagne flute
and top with the chilled Champagne. Garnish with
the cherries.

Adam's Apple

1 apple slice or small apple wedge
$1/_3$ oz (10 ml) Calvados
Champagne, chilled

Place the apple slice or wedge in a champagne flute.
Add the Calvados and top with the chilled Champagne.

One-five-one

1 sugar cube
Dash of sour cherry syrup
1 oz (30 ml) Bacardi 151 rum
Champagne, chilled

Place the sugar cube in a champagne flute and pour
the cherry syrup over. Add the rum and top with the
chilled Champagne.

RIGHT:Croatian Cherry (left),
Adam's Apple (middle), One-five-one (right)

Martinis

The origins of the martini are as shrouded in mystery as the origins of the cocktail itself. Some say it first appeared in New York, others favor San Francisco. More likely is that it was named for the Martini & Rossi company, makers of the famous vermouth.

Regardless of its origins, there's no doubting that the classic gin and vermouth martini has spawned more variations than just about any other drink on the planet. Thanks to the martini's great fertility, you may now never have the same martini twice, but, in the proper hands, you can have a superb martini every time. In this book, we've gone for vodka as the "parent" element for our martinis. The popularity of vodka in recent times has seen it overtake gin as the preferred base, and it still imparts the classic lightness and dryness that epitomize the martini.

Whether you're keeping an eye on the bartender or mixing them at home, make sure your martini is served in a chilled martini or cocktail glass. It's even a good idea to keep a few glasses in the freezer for when those unexpected guests drop in. Remember to always consume this tipple immediately, while it's still icy cold—a quick drink also gives you a legitimate excuse for a second round!

Scud Martini

Ice cubes
3 oz (90 ml) chili-infused vodka
1 small fresh red chili and 1 green olive, to garnish

Half fill a cocktail shaker with the ice cubes and add the vodka, then stir and strain into a chilled martini glass. Garnish with the chili and olive.

Killer Martini

Ice cubes
3 oz (90 ml) vodka
1 pimiento-stuffed green olive and 1 teaspoon blue cheese, to garnish

Half fill a cocktail shaker with the ice cubes and add the vodka, then stir and strain into a chilled martini glass. Remove the pimiento from the olive and fill the center of the olive with the blue cheese. Garnish the martini with the blue cheese-stuffed olive.

RIGHT: Scud Martini
PAGE 7: Killer Martini

Rose Water Cinnamon Martini

Ice cubes
3 oz (90 ml) vodka
$1/_3$ oz (10 ml) rose water
1 cinnamon stick, to garnish

Half fill a cocktail shaker with the ice cubes and add the vodka and rose water. Stir and strain the mixture into a chilled martini glass and garnish with the cinnamon stick.

Hazelnut Martini

Ice cubes
3 oz (90 ml) vodka
$1/_2$ oz (15 ml) Frangelico
6 almond slices, toasted, to garnish

Half fill a cocktail shaker with the ice cubes and add the vodka and Frangelico. Stir and strain the mixture into a chilled martini glass and garnish with the almond slices.

Crown Martini

Ice cubes
$1/_3$ oz (10 ml) Chambord
1 oz (30 ml) vodka
$1/_2$ oz (15 ml) fresh lemon juice
$1/_2$ oz (15 ml) grapefruit juice

Half fill a cocktail shaker with the ice cubes and add the Chambord, vodka and juices. Stir and strain the mixture into a chilled martini glass.

Apple Martini

Ice cubes
2 oz (60 ml) vodka
2 oz (60 ml) Calvados
1 thin slice apple, to garnish

Half fill a cocktail shaker with the ice cubes and add the vodka and Calvados. Stir and strain the mixture into a chilled large martini glass and garnish with the apple slice.

RIGHT: Rose Water Cinnamon Martini (front)
Hazelnut Martini (back)

Audience Martini

Ice cubes
3 oz (90 ml) gin
Dash of orange bitters
Splash of blood orange juice
1 grapefruit twist, to garnish

Half fill a cocktail shaker with the ice cubes and add the gin, orange bitters and juice. Stir and strain the mixture into a chilled martini glass and garnish with the grapefruit twist.

Berry Martini

Ice cubes
2 oz (60 ml) vodka
1 oz (30 ml) eau-de-vie framboise
  sauvage or eau-de-vie de fraise
1 fresh raspberry or strawberry,
  to garnish

Half fill a cocktail shaker with the ice cubes and add the vodka and eau-de-vie. Stir and strain the mixture into a chilled martini glass and garnish with the raspberry or strawberry.

Honey Martini

Ice cubes
2 oz (60 ml) vodka
1 oz (30 ml) Old Krupnik
1 tangerine (mandarin orange)
  twist, to garnish

Half fill a cocktail shaker with the ice cubes and add the vodka and Old Krupnik. Stir and strain the mixture into a chilled martini glass and garnish with the tangerine twist.

Vanilla Martini

Ice cubes
2 oz (60 ml) vodka
$1/_2$ oz (15 ml) Licor 43
1 vanilla bean, to garnish

Half fill a cocktail shaker with the ice cubes and add the vodka and Licor 43. Stir and strain the mixture into a chilled martini glass and place the vanilla bean in the martini, resting across the glass.

LEFT: Audience Martini

Watermelon Martini

Ice cubes
$1^1/_2$ oz (45 ml) vodka
2 oz (60 ml) watermelon juice
Dash of sugar syrup
1 small slice watermelon, to garnish

Half fill a cocktail shaker with the ice cubes and add the vodka, watermelon juice and sugar syrup. Stir and strain the mixture into a chilled martini glass and garnish with the watermelon slice.

Sake Martini

Ice cubes
1 oz (30 ml) sake
1 oz (30 ml) vodka
Dash of gin
1 slice cucumber, to garnish

Half fill a cocktail shaker with the ice cubes and add the sake, vodka and gin. Stir and strain the mixture into a chilled martini glass and garnish with the cucumber slice.

Beetle

Ice cubes
1 oz (30 ml) vodka
1 oz (30 ml) Chartreuse
$^1/_2$ oz (15 ml) Triple Sec

Half fill a cocktail shaker with the ice cubes and add the vodka, Chartreuse and Triple Sec, then stir and strain into a chilled martini glass.

Lemon Warhead

Ice cubes
3 oz (90 ml) Absolut Citron vodka
Dash of Angostura bitters
1 lemon twist, to garnish

Half fill a cocktail shaker with the ice cubes and add the vodka and bitters. Stir and strain the mixture into a chilled martini glass and garnish with the lemon twist.

Strange Keys

Ice cubes
2 orange quarters
2 oz (60 ml) sloe gin
$^1/_2$ oz (15 ml) Cognac

Half fill a cocktail shaker with the ice cubes and squeeze the orange pieces over the ice. Add the sloe gin and Cognac, then stir and strain into a chilled martini glass.

RIGHT: Watermelon Martini

Blended Cocktails

Now there's a plea for a blended cocktail if ever there was one! Emerson knew a thing or two about quality, even if he may not have been thinking about cocktails on this occasion. But his observation is no less applicable: the freshest of fruit and good-quality ice are essential for the success of a blended cocktail.

In fact, blending is one of the easiest methods of mixing a cocktail. All you do is combine ice cubes, fruit, alcohol and sometimes cream, in a blender. A blender is essential for these cocktails. If you don't already have one, be sure to invest in a good quality model. One that's strong enough to crush ice (look for one with a 400–500-watt motor); check the user manual to be sure it's suitable for this use.

Choose a blender with a glass container. That way you can enjoy watching the colors come together. And make sure it has a tight-fitting lid, so you don't end up with more liquid on the floor than in the glass. Ideally, it should also have a pouring spout or lip.

One last tip on the subject of ice: don't use tap water, which can contain any number of vile-tasting "purifiers," or cubes that have served time in the same cell as other foods and so have absorbed some of their neighbors' odors. Good-quality bottled water, preferably spring water, is best. Freeze it into cubes as close to cocktail preparation time as possible. You won't believe what a difference it makes to the taste.

Grand Mango

1 oz (30 ml) mango purée
1 oz (30 ml) Campari
1$^1/_2$ oz (45 ml) Grand Marnier
$^1/_2$ cup (75 g) ice cubes

Pour the mango purée into a chilled cocktail or martini glass. Combine the Campari, Grand Marnier and ice cubes in a blender and process until smooth, then pour into the glass with the mango purée.

Berry Splice

1/2 cup (75 g) ice cubes
1/2 oz (15 ml) Baileys Irish Cream
1/2 oz (15 ml) framboise
1/2 oz (15 ml) crème de cacao
1/2 oz (15 ml) Kahlúa
1/4 cup (60 ml) half-and-half
  cream (half milk, half cream)
5 fresh strawberries, hulled
1 oz (30 ml) crème de mûre

Process the ice cubes, Baileys Irish cream, framboise, crème de cacao, Kahlúa, half-and-half cream and 4 strawberries in a blender until smooth. Pour the crème de mûre into a chilled cocktail glass, then pour the processed mixture over the back of a spoon to layer it over the crème de mûre. Garnish with the remaining strawberry.

Slivovitz Plum Daiquiri

1/2 cup (75 g) ice cubes
2 oz (60 ml) slivovitz
1/3 oz (10 ml) Cointreau
1/3 oz (10 ml) fresh lemon juice
3 fresh plums, peeled and pitted,
  or 3 canned plums, drained
1 fresh strawberry, to garnish

Process the ice cubes, slivovitz, Cointreau, lemon juice and plums in a blender until smooth. Pour the processed mixture into a chilled cocktail or martini glass and garnish with the strawberry.

Candy Pop

1 cup (150 g) ice cubes
1/2 oz (15 ml) peach schnapps
1/2 oz (15 ml) apple schnapps
1/2 oz (15 ml) strawberry liqueur
2 oz (60 ml) fresh lemon juice
1 oz (30 ml) orange juice
1 fresh strawberry and 1 lime
  twist, to garnish

Process the ice cubes, schnapps, liqueur and juices in a blender until smooth, then pour into a chilled cocktail or martini glass and garnish with the strawberry and lime twist.

RIGHT: Berry Splice

Caper and Chili Juice

6 ice cubes
2 oz (60 ml) vodka
1 small fresh red chili, deseeded
1 small ripe tomato, deseeded
Dash of Worcestershire sauce
Dash of Tabasco sauce
6 capers
Ground white pepper
1 cucumber stick, to garnish

Process all the ingredients, except the pepper and garnish, in a blender until smooth. Pour the processed mixture into a white pepper-rimmed margarita or large martini glass and garnish with the cucumber stick.

Honeydew and Kiwifruit Daiquiri

$1/_2$ cup (90 g) chopped honeydew
1 kiwifruit, peeled and chopped
2 oz (60 ml) Bacardi white rum
$1/_2$ oz (15 ml) fresh lemon juice
$1/_2$ oz (15 ml) sugar syrup
Sugar
1 sprig fresh mint, to garnish

Process all the ingredients, except the sugar and garnish, in a blender until smooth. Pour the processed mixture into a sugar-rimmed margarita or large martini glass and garnish with the mint sprig.

Banana and Pineapple Refresher

5 fresh strawberries, hulled
Dash of sugar syrup
$1/_2$ cup (75 g) ice cubes
$1/_2$ oz (15 ml) white rum
$1/_2$ cup (90 g) chopped pineapple
$1/_2$ banana, peeled and chopped
1 lime, peeled
2 fresh mint leaves
1 strawberry slice, to garnish

1 Process the strawberries and sugar syrup in a blender until smooth, and pour into a chilled cocktail or large martini glass.
2 Rinse the blender well, then process the ice cubes, white rum, pineapple, banana, limes and mint. Pour the processed mixture over the strawberry purée and garnish with the strawberry slice.

LEFT: Caper and Chili Juice

Sgroppino

1 scoop lemon sorbet
2 oz (60 ml) prosecco
1 lemon slice, to garnish

Process the sorbet and prosecco in a blender until smooth and pour into a chilled old-fashioned glass. Garnish with the lemon slice.

Golden Banana

$^1/_2$ cup (75 g) ice cubes
2 oz (60 ml) Jamaican rum
$^1/_2$ banana, peeled and chopped
1 teaspoon vanilla extract
1 lemon wedge, to garnish

Process all the ingredients, except the garnish, in a blender until smooth. Pour the processed mixture into a chilled cocktail or martini glass and garnish with the lemon wedge.

Banana Fizz

$^1/_2$ banana, peeled and chopped
$^1/_2$ cup (75 g) ice cubes
1 oz (30 ml) vodka
$^1/_2$ oz (15 ml) banana liqueur
$^1/_2$ oz (15 ml) fresh lemon juice
Lemonade or soda water, chilled
  (optional)
1 fresh blossom, to garnish

Process the banana, ice cubes, vodka, banana liqueur and lemon juice in a blender until smooth. Pour the processed mixture into a chilled cocktail or large martini glass, then top with the chilled lemonade or soda water if desired and garnish with the fresh blossom.

LEFT: Sgroppino

Fruit Daiquiris

$1/_2$ cup (75 g) ice cubes
1 cup (125 g) chopped fresh
  mango, banana, whole strawberries, raspberries, lychees or
  boysenberries
2 oz (60 ml) Bacardi white rum
1 oz (30 ml) flavored liqueur
  (specific to fruit chosen)
$1/_3$ oz (10 ml) fresh lemon juice
Fresh fruit slices or berries,
  to garnish

Process the ice cubes, fruit, rum, liqueur and lemon juice in a blender until smooth. Pour the processed mixture into a chilled cocktail or martini glass and garnish with slices of fruit or berries.

Berry Surprise

$1/_2$ cup (75 g) ice cubes
1 oz (30 ml) vodka
$1/_2$ oz (15 ml) raspberry liqueur
1 oz (30 ml) grapefruit juice
1 oz (30 ml) cranberry juice
1 oz (30 ml) blackcurrant juice
$1/_4$ oz ($7^1/_2$ ml) blue curaçao
3 fresh or canned peach wedges
1 fresh peach wedge, to garnish

Process all the ingredients, except the garnish, in a blender until smooth. Pour the processed mixture into a chilled cocktail or martini glass and garnish with the remaining peach wedge.

RIGHT: Boysenberry Daiquiris (back),
Strawberry Daiquiris (front)

Coconut Holiday

1 cup (150 g) ice cubes
1$^1/_2$ oz (45 ml) dark rum
1 oz (30 ml) pineapple juice
1 oz (30 ml) orange juice
1 oz (30 ml) cranberry juice
1 oz (30 ml) coconut cream
Fresh pineapple leaves, to garnish

Process all the ingredients, except the garnish, in a blender until smooth. Pour the processed mixture into a highball glass and garnish with the pineapple leaves.

Pear Daiquiri

1 cup (150 g) ice cubes
1 oz (30 ml) Bacardi white rum
1 oz (30 ml) Poire William
$^1/_2$ poached or canned pear
1 teaspoon fresh lemon juice
1 fresh blossom, to garnish

Process all the ingredients, except the garnish, in a blender until smooth. Pour the processed mixture into a chilled cocktail or martini glass and garnish with the blossom.

RIGHT: Mango Daiquiri
(see page 56 for recipe)

Crushed Cocktails

The preparation of so-called "crushed" cocktails or "stick drinks" gives you an opportunity to employ that most unappetizing of verbs, "to muddle". "I'll just go and muddle the mint leaves and sugar," you can tell your bemused guests, as you slip behind the bar or head for the kitchen to prepare that mint julep. Professional mixologists, of course, are never caught without their muddler—a wooden stick with a flattened end—used to mash ingredients together to slowly release their flavors.

If you have got a muddler, you'll appreciate how its wooden end won't scratch the glass. If you don't have one, use the back of a spoon, the end of a rolling pin or a pestle to crush the ingredients against the base and side of the serving glass, not forgetting to first wrap a towel around the glass to prevent it breaking in mid-muddle. Use a mortar and pestle if you're preparing more than one drink of this kind. Your blender can provide crushed ice. If it's not up to the job, try this: put the ice cubes in a sealable plastic bag, cover with a towel and bash with a meat tenderizer. Don't apply too much force, though, or you'll tear the towel. Unwrap, unzip and transfer to the waiting glasses. Crushed cocktails are generally served in old-fashioned or highball glasses.

Passion Fruit Caipiroska

1 lime, quartered
Pulp of 1 passionfruit
Ice cubes
2 oz (60 ml) vodka
1 oz (30 ml) passionfruit liqueur
1 fresh blossom, to garnish

Place the lime quarters in an old-fashioned glass and muddle until the juice is extracted. Add the passionfruit pulp and fill the glass with some ice cubes. Pour the vodka and passionfruit liqueur over the ice and stir well. Garnish with the fresh blossom.

Note: For Lychee Caipiroska, use fresh lychee and lychee licqueur in place of the passionfruit pulp and passionfruit liqueur.

Blood Orange Crush

Crushed ice
1$^1/_2$ oz (45 ml) Campari
$^1/_2$ oz (15 ml) Cointreau
Blood orange juice, chilled
Ruby red grapefruit juice
Ruby red grapefruit wedge,
  to garnish

Fill an old-fashioned glass with some crushed ice.
Add the Campari and Cointreau, and top with equal
amounts of the blood orange juice and grapefruit juice.
Garnish with the ruby red grapefruit wedge.

Caiperol

1 lime, cut into eighths
3 sugar cubes
Ice cubes
2 oz (60 ml) Aperol

Place the lime wedges and sugar in a highball glass,
and muddle until the juice is extracted and the sugar is
crushed. Fill the glass with some ice cubes, add the
Aperol and stir.

Tangerine Cooler

6 fresh mint leaves
1 sugar cube
1 tangerine (mandarin orange),
  cut into wedges
Ice cubes
1 oz (30 ml) Absolut Citron vodka
1 oz (30 ml) cranberry juice, chilled

Place the mint leaves and sugar cube in a highball
glass and muddle until the sugar is crushed. Add the
tangerine wedges and continue to muddle until the
juice is extracted. Fill the glass with some ice cubes,
add the vodka and cranberry juice, and stir.

Apple Man

$^1/_2$ apple, peeled, cored and
  chopped, plus 1 apple wedge
  to garnish
Ice cubes
1 oz (30 ml) vodka
1 oz (30 ml) gin
1 oz (30 ml) Calvados
Soda water, chilled
1 apple wedge, for garnish

Place the chopped apple in a highball glass and muddle
until crushed, then fill the glass with some ice cubes.
Add the vodka, gin and Calvados, top with the chilled
soda and stir. Garnish with the apple wedge.

RIGHT: Blood orange Crush

Pine Lime Crush

Crushed ice
4 lime wedges
2 oz (60 ml) vodka
Pineapple juice, chilled

Fill an old-fashioned glass with some crushed ice and squeeze the lime wedges over the ice. Add the lime peels to the glass and pour in the vodka. Top with the pineapple juice and stir.

Caipiroska

1 lime, cut into eighths
3 sugar cubes
Ice cubes
2 oz (60 ml) vodka

Place the lime wedges and sugar in a highball glass and muddle until the juice is extracted and the sugar is crushed. Fill the glass with some ice cubes, add the vodka and stir.

Berry Caipiroska

2 lime quarters
2 fresh blueberries
2 fresh raspberries
3 fresh strawberries, hulled
4 ruby red grapefruit juice ice cubes
2 oz (60 ml) vodka
$1/_2$ oz (15 ml) framboise

Place the lime quarters, blueberries, raspberries and 2 strawberries in an old-fashioned glass, and muddle until the berries are crushed. Add the grapefruit juice ice cubes, pour the vodka and framboise over the ice and stir. Garnish with the remaining strawberry.

Grapefruit Caipiroska

2 grapefruit wedges, peels discarded, chopped
2 lime wedges
Ice cubes
$1^1/_2$ oz (45 ml) Absolut Kurant vodka
$1/_2$ oz (15 ml) crème de mûre
Ruby red grapefruit juice, chilled
1 grapefruit twist, to garnish

Place the grapefruit flesh and lime wedges in an old-fashioned glass and muddle until the juice is extracted. Fill the glass with some ice cubes and add the vodka and crème de mûre. Top with the grapefruit juice and stir. Garnish with the grapefruit twist.

LEFT: Pine Lime Crush

Gin Club

4 fresh mint leaves, plus extra
  mint leaves to garnish
3 sugar cubes
Ice cubes
2 oz (60 ml) gin
$1/2$ oz (15 ml) Aperol

Place the mint leaves and sugar in a highball glass and muddle until the sugar is crushed. Fill the glass with some ice cubes, add the gin and Aperol, and stir. Garnish with the extra mint leaves, if desired.

Eau de Coing

Crushed ice
1 oz (30 ml) quince liqueur
1 oz (30 ml) Frangelico
Blood orange juice, chilled
Fresh mint leaves, to garnish

Fill a highball glass with some crushed ice and add the quince liqueur and Frangelico, then top with the orange juice and stir. Garnish with the mint leaves.

Ginger Mojito

1 teaspoon grated fresh ginger root
1 lime, cut into wedges
6 fresh mint leaves, plus extra
  mint leaves to garnish
1 teaspoon sugar
Ice cubes
2 oz (60 ml) golden rum
Soda water, chilled

Place the ginger, lime, mint leaves and sugar in an old-fashioned glass and muddle until the juice is extracted and the sugar is crushed. Fill the glass with some ice cubes and add the rum, then top with the chilled soda and stir. Garnish with the extra mint leaves.

Jaggard Crush

Crushed ice
4 lime quarters
1 oz (30 ml) Jaggard Original
1 oz (30 ml) Cointreau
$1/2$ oz (15 ml) Absolut Citron vodka
$1/2$ oz (15 ml) Absolut Kurant vodka
Ruby red grapefruit juice, chilled
1 ruby red grapefruit wedge,
  to garnish

Fill a highball glass with some crushed ice and squeeze the lime quarters over the ice. Add the lime peels to the glass and pour in the Jaggard, Cointreau and vodkas. Top with the grapefruit juice and garnish with the grapefruit wedge.

RIGHT: Gin Club

Built Cocktails

In our case, an edifice of ice—whole or crushed—alcohol, juice and decoration. As for rebuilding it every day all you need to do is quote André Maurois and you have the perfect excuse for creating one of these fabulous thirst-quenchers day in, day out.

Yes, built cocktails are meant for slaking the parched throat, rather than for slow sipping. And don't they look good! The Japanese say that food should look good as well as taste good. So should cocktails, and here's the proof.

Built cocktails are among the simplest around and require the minimum of equipment. All you do is take a highball or old-fashioned glass, fill it with ice (from bottled water, of course), then the liquid ingredients. Give the lot a slow stir with a long bar spoon so the flavors blend gently with each other. As a final touch, let your imagination go wild and decorate the drink with garnishes of fruit, lime or orange zest, even pineapple leaves.

Blackberry Emergency

Ice cubes
$1/_2$ oz (15 ml) Absolut Citron vodka
$1/_2$ oz (15 ml) Absolut Kurant vodka
$1/_3$ oz (10 ml) crème de cassis
$1/_3$ oz (10 ml) Triple Sec
$1/_4$ oz ($7^1/_2$ ml) fresh lime juice
Cranberry juice, chilled
1 lime twist, to garnish

Fill a highball glass with some ice cubes and add the vodkas, crème de cassis, Triple Sec and lime juice. Top with the cranberry juice and stir, then garnish with the lime twist.

Ginger Melon

Ice cubes
$1^1/_2$ oz (45 ml) Absolut Citron
  vodka
$^1/_2$ oz (15 ml) Cointreau
$^1/_2$ oz (15 ml) ginger liqueur
3 oz (90 ml) watermelon juice
1 orange wedge, to garnish

Fill a highball glass with some ice cubes. Add the vodka, Cointreau, ginger liqueur and watermelon juice and stir. Garnish with the orange wedge.

Pisco Sour

Ice cubes
2 oz (60 ml) pisco
2 oz (60 ml) fresh lime juice
Dash of sugar syrup
1 lime twist, to garnish

Fill an old-fashioned glass with some ice cubes. Add the pisco, lime juice and sugar syrup, and stir. Garnish with the lime twist.

Soda and Citrus

Ice cubes
1 oz (30 ml) peach schnapps
1 oz (30 ml) fresh lime juice
1 oz (30 ml) grapefruit juice
Soda water, chilled
1 peach wedge, to garnish

Fill a highball glass with some ice cubes and add the peach schnapps and juices. Top with the chilled soda and stir. Garnish with the peach wedge.

LEFT: Ginger Melon

Ginger "n" Orange

Ice cubes
3 orange wedges
Fresh orange juice, chilled
$1/_2$ oz (15 ml) fresh ginger juice
1 oz (30 ml) vodka
Ginger ale, chilled
1 mint leaf, to garnish

Combine some ice cubes and the orange wedges in an old-fashioned glass, then fill the glass one-third full with the orange juice. Add the ginger juice and vodka, top with the chilled ginger ale and stir. Garnish with the mint leaf.

Tiberian Sun

Ice cubes
$1^1/_2$ oz (45 ml) Absolut Citron vodka
$1/_2$ oz (15 ml) Cointreau
$1/_2$ oz (15 ml) crème de mûre
1 teaspoon puréed boysenberries
Pear juice, chilled
2 lime wedges, to garnish

Fill a highball glass with some ice cubes and add the vodka, Cointreau, crème de mûre and boysenberry purée. Top with the pear juice and stir. Garnish with the lime wedges.

Soda Nut

Ice cubes
$1/_2$ oz (15 ml) amaretto
2 oz (60 ml) fresh orange juice
2 oz (60 ml) chilled soda water
1 orange twist, to garnish

Fill a highball glass with some ice cubes and add the amaretto and orange juice. Top with the chilled soda water and stir. Garnish with the orange twist.

RIGHT: Ginger "n" Orange

Lifesaver

Ice cubes
1 oz (30 ml) raspberry liqueur
1 oz (30 ml) gin
2 oz (60 ml) guava nectar
Dash of Angostura bitters
Pineapple leaves, to garnish

Fill a highball glass with some ice cubes. Add the raspberry liqueur, gin, guava nectar and bitters, and stir. Garnish with the pineapple leaves.

Sunshine

Crushed ice
1 oz (30 ml) dark rum
$1/2$ oz (15 ml) Cointreau
1 oz (30 ml) apricot nectar
1 oz (30 ml) tangerine (mandarin
  orange) juice
$1/4$ oz ($7^1/2$ ml) fresh lime juice
1 orange twist, to garnish

Fill a large martini glass with some crushed ice. Add the rum, Cointreau, apricot nectar and juices, and stir. Garnish with the orange twist.

King

Ice cubes
1 oz (30 ml) brandy
$1/2$ oz (15 ml) fresh lemon juice
$1/2$ oz (15 ml) fresh lime juice
Soda water, chilled
1 lime wedge, to garnish

Fill a highball glass with some ice cubes and add the brandy and juices. Top with the chilled soda water and stir. Garnish with the lime wedge.

Ginger and Mandarin Sea Breeze

Ice cubes
$1/2$ oz (15 ml) ginger liqueur
$1/2$ oz (15 ml) Absolut Mandarin
  vodka
3 cranberry juice ice cubes
1 oz (30 ml) grapefruit juice
1 lime wedge, to garnish

Fill a highball glass with some ice cubes. Add the ginger liqueur, vodka, cranberry juice ice cubes and grapefruit juice, and stir. Garnish with the lime wedge.

LEFT: Lifesaver

Wild Strawberries

Ice cubes
3 fresh strawberries, hulled
1 oz (30 ml) fraise des bois
1 oz (30 ml) light rum
Squeeze of lemon juice
Soda water or lemonade, chilled

Fill a highball glass with some ice cubes and add the strawberries, fraise des bois, rum and lemon juice. Top with the chilled soda water or lemonade and stir.

Gingerene

Crushed ice
1 oz (30 ml) gin
1 oz (30 ml) ginger liqueur
1 oz (30 ml) golden rum
3 lime juice ice cubes
1 oz (30 ml) tangerine (mandarin
  orange) juice
1 tangerine (mandarin orange)
  wedge, to garnish

Fill a large martini glass with some crushed ice. Add the gin, ginger liqueur, rum, lime juice ice cubes and orange juice, and stir. Garnish with orange wedge.

Cranberry Apple Sour

Ice cubes
1 oz (30 ml) apple schnapps
1 oz (30 ml) fresh lime juice
2 oz (60 ml) cranberry juice
Splash of Bacardi 151 rum
1 lime wedge, to garnish

Fill a highball glass with some ice cubes, add the apple schnapps, juices and rum, and stir. Garnish with the lime wedge.

RIGHT: Wild Strawberries

Guava Vogue

Ice cubes
1 oz (30 ml) tequila
1 oz (30 ml) Cointreau
1 oz (30 ml) guava juice
1 oz (30 ml) fresh lime juice
Soda water, chilled
1 papaya wedge and lime zest,
    to garnish

Fill a highball glass with some ice cubes and add the tequila, Cointreau and juices. Top with the chilled soda water and stir. Garnish with the papaya wedge and lime zest.

Napoleon

Ice cubes
1 oz (30 ml) Mandarin Napoleon
$^1/_4$ oz ($7^1/_2$ ml) Cointreau
1 oz (30 ml) fresh lime juice
3 orange juice ice cubes
1 lime twist, to garnish

Fill a highball glass with some ice cubes, add the Mandarin Napoleon, Cointreau, lime juice and orange juice ice cubes, and stir. Garnish with the lime twist.

Citrus Fountain

Crushed ice
2 oz (60 ml) Absolut Mandarin
    vodka
1 oz (30 ml) Cognac
1 oz (30 ml) grapefruit juice
1 oz (30 ml) orange juice
1 oz (30 ml) fresh lime juice
1 grapefruit wedge, to garnish

Fill a large martini glass with some crushed ice, add the vodka, Cognac and juices, and stir. Garnish with the grapefruit wedge.

LEFT: Guava Vogue

Shaken and Strained Cocktails

We've all heard James Bond's preference for "shaken, not stirred." Shaken cocktails are by far the most impressive and fun to watch. Remember the movie Cocktail with Tom Cruise and Bryan Brown? But why restrict your enjoyment to the silver screen or watching cocktail-bartenders hurling shakers about like circus stars. You can get more kicks by doing it yourself at home or at a party. Just make sure the lid's firmly attached!

Here are the rules:

1. Keep the shaker, whether metal or glass, in the freezer until you need it.

2. Fill the shaker with ice cubes before you add your chosen cocktail ingredients.

3. Shaking means vigorous blending, so shake with a good, steady rhythm. Put on some music and shake to the beat.

4. Shake only one drink at a time. That way you get to repeat the performance. You never know—there might be a talent scout somewhere in the audience.

5. Remove the lid with a flourish and strain the drink into a chilled cocktail glass. If your shaker comes with a strainer, use that. If not, here's your chance to use that professional strainer some hopeful friend gave you last birthday.

6. Garnish your masterpiece, sit back and enjoy. Or present it to your guests before whipping one up "for the cook."

Cherry Tree

Ice cubes
1 oz (30 ml) cherry liqueur
1 oz (30 ml) Calvados
1 oz (30 ml) fresh lemon juice
1 oz (30 ml) fresh lime juice

Fill a highball glass and a cocktail shaker with some ice cubes. Add the cherry liqueur, Calvados and juices to the shaker, then shake and strain the mixture into the ice-filled glass.

Tangerine Sour

Ice cubes
2 oz (60 ml) pisco
1 oz (30 ml) tangerine (mandarin orange) juice
1 oz (30 ml) fresh lime juice
Dash of lightly beaten egg white
1 tangerine (mandarin orange) wedge, to garnish

Fill a cocktail shaker with some ice cubes and add the pisco, juices and egg white. Shake and strain the mixture into a large martini glass and garnish with the tangerine wedge.

Raspberry Collins

Ice cubes
2 oz (60 ml) vodka
$1/_2$ oz (15 ml) fresh lemon juice
1 oz (30 ml) framboise
2 teaspoons raspberry purée
Soda water, chilled

Fill a highball glass and cocktail shaker with some ice cubes. Add the vodka, lemon juice, framboise and raspberry purée to the shaker, and shake and strain the mixture into the ice-filled glass. Top with the chilled soda.

Raspberry Sourgear

Ice cubes
1 oz (30 ml) gin
$1/_2$ oz (15 ml) Monin Lime
Natural mineral water with orange
  juice
$1/_2$ oz (15 ml) raspberry liqueur

Fill a highball glass and cocktail shaker with some ice cubes. Add the gin and Monin Lime to the shaker, then shake and strain the mixture into the ice-filled glass. Top with the mineral water with orange juice, followed by the raspberry liqueur.

Green Fairy

Ice cubes
1 oz (30 ml) absinthe or Pernod
1 oz (30 ml) Cointreau
1 oz (30 ml) fresh lime juice
1 teaspoon honey
1 orange slice, to garnish

Fill a cocktail shaker with some ice cubes, then add the absinthe or Pernod, Cointreau, lime juice and honey. Shake and strain the mixture into a champagne saucer, and garnish with the orange slice.

Margarita No. 5

Ice cubes
2 oz (60 ml) tequila
1 oz (30 ml) Cointreau
$1/_3$ oz (10 ml) fresh lemon juice
$1/_2$ oz (15 ml) ruby red grapefruit
  juice
$1/_2$ oz (15 ml) orange juice
$1/_2$ oz (15 ml) fresh lime juice
$1/_2$ oz (15 ml) blood orange juice
Dash of lightly beaten egg white
Sugar

Fill a cocktail shaker with some ice cubes and add the tequila, Cointreau, juices and egg white. Shake and strain the mixture into a sugar-rimmed large martini or margarita glass.

RIGHT: Raspberry Collins

Strawberry Hills

Ice cubes
1$^1/_2$ oz (45 ml) tequila
$^1/_2$ oz (15 ml) Triple Sec
$^1/_2$ oz (15 ml) fresh lime juice
2 teaspoons strawberry purée
Dash of strawberry liqueur

Fill a cocktail shaker with some ice cubes and add the tequila, Triple Sec, lime juice, strawberry purée and strawberry liqueur. Shake and strain the mixture into a cocktail glass or wineglass.

Peach Apricot Shaker

Ice cubes
1 oz (30 ml) gin
1 oz (30 ml) Cointreau
1 oz (30 ml) apricot nectar
1 oz (30 ml) peach nectar
$^1/_2$ oz (15 ml) grapefruit juice
Sugar

Fill a cocktail shaker with some ice cubes and add the gin, Cointreau, nectars and grapefruit juice. Shake and strain the mixture into a sugar-rimmed large martini glass.

Spitfire

Ice cubes
2 oz (60 ml) gin
1 oz (30 ml) Cointreau
2 oz (60 ml) ruby red grapefruit
  juice
Dash of Angostura bitters
Dash of sugar syrup
Dash of lightly beaten egg white

Fill a cocktail shaker with some ice cubes and add the gin, Cointreau, grapefruit juice, bitters, sugar syrup and egg white. Shake and strain the mixture into a large martini glass.

Blood Berries

Ice cubes
$^1/_2$ oz (15 ml) Chambord
$^1/_2$ oz (15 ml) vodka
1 oz (30 ml) blood orange juice
1 oz (30 ml) cranberry juice

Fill a cocktail shaker with some ice cubes and add the Chambord, vodka and juices. Shake and strain the mixture into a large martini glass.

LEFT: Strawberry Hills

Sour Morning

1 long strip orange zest
Ice cubes
$^1/_2$ oz (15 ml) vodka
Dash of Angostura bitters
2 oz (60 ml) grapefruit juice
2 oz (60 ml) ruby red grapefruit
  juice
2 oz (60 ml) blood orange juice
1 oz (30 ml) fresh lemon juice
1 oz (30 ml) fresh lime juice

1 Wind the strip of orange zest into an old-fashioned glass and add some ice cubes.
2 Fill a cocktail shaker with some ice cubes and add the vodka, bitters and juices. Shake and strain the mixture into the ice-filled glass.

Blanc

Ice cubes
1 oz (30 ml) gin
1 oz (30 ml) fresh lime juice
1 oz (30 ml) Cointreau
1 oz (30 ml) Lillet Blanc
1 lime wedge, to garnish

Fill a cocktail shaker with some ice cubes and add the gin, lime juice, Cointreau and Lillet Blanc. Shake and strain the mixture into a large martini glass, and garnish with the lime wedge.

Pimms Green Tea Refresher

Long thin cucumber slices (made
  with a vegetable peeler)
Ice cubes
2 oz (60 ml) Pimms
$^1/_2$ oz (15 ml) Monin Lime
1 cup (250 ml) cold green tea

1 Arrange the cucumber slices in a highball glass and add some ice cubes.
2 Fill a cocktail shaker with some ice cubes and add the Pimms, Monin Lime and cold tea. Shake and strain the mixture into the ice-filled glass.

Verbs

Ice cubes
1 oz (30 ml) lemon verbena liqueur
1 oz (30 ml) pisco
2 oz (60 ml) blood orange juice
1 orange wedge, to garnish

Fill a cocktail shaker with some ice cubes and add the liqueur, pisco and orange juice. Shake and strain the mixture into a large martini glass, and garnish with the orange wedge.

RIGHT: Sour Morning

Nonalcoholic Cocktails

If you want the fun without the hangover, there are loads of nonalcoholic cocktails that look just like the real thing and still allow you to drive home safely.

And because you can dress up these combos with colorful garnishes in glasses with frosted rims, they're sure to be popular with kids keen to strut their sophistication. Just dip the rim of the glass in beaten egg white, then sugar or salt, before filling it up with freshly juiced fruits or vegetables of choice. Do you know a sneakier way of getting them to take their vitamins?

Tutti Frutti

6 fresh strawberries, hulled
$1/2$ cup (75 g) ice cubes
$1/2$ oz (15 ml) apricot juice
$1/2$ oz (15 ml) pineapple juice
$1/2$ oz (15 ml) ruby red grapefruit juice
$1/2$ oz (15 ml) cranberry juice
$1/2$ oz (15 ml) orange juice
$1/2$ oz (15 ml) fresh lemon juice
$1/2$ mango, peeled and pitted, chopped
1 ruby red grapefruit wedge, to garnish

Process the strawberries in a blender until smooth and pour into a champagne saucer. Rinse the blender and process the ice cubes, all the juices and chopped mango to a purée, then pour the processed mixture over the strawberry purée. Garnish with the grapefruit wedge.

Crenshaw

Ice cubes
2 oz (60 ml) cranberry juice
1 oz (30 ml) ruby red grapefruit juice
Dash of pineapple juice
$1/2$ oz (15 ml) sour cherry syrup
Dash of Angostura bitters
1 orange wedge

Fill a highball glass with some ice cubes, add the juices, syrup and bitters, and stir. Squeeze the orange wedge over the mixture and garnish with the orange peel.

LEFT: Tutti Frutti

Ginger Peach Punch

1 cup (150 g) ice cubes
2 cups (500 ml) peach nectar, chilled
$1/_4$ cup (60 ml) fresh lime juice
2 peaches, peeled, pitted and sliced
$1/_4$ cup (60 ml) ginger syrup
4 cups (1 liter) ginger beer, chilled
1 lime, thinly sliced, to garnish
8 fresh mint leaves, to garnish

Combine the ice cubes, peach nectar, lime juice, peaches, ginger syrup and beer in a large glass bowl and stir. Garnish with the lime slices and mint leaves.

Note: To make this into an alcoholic punch, add 6 oz (180 ml) of dark rum.

Serves 6

Tropicana

1 cup (150 g) ice cubes
$1/_2$ cup (125 ml) pineapple juice
$1/_2$ oz (15 ml) lychee juice
$1/_4$ cup (45 g) chopped papaya
$1/_2$ cup (90 g) chopped mango
2 fresh mint leaves, to garnish

Process the ice cubes, juices, papaya and mango in a blender until smooth. Pour the processed mixture into a large cocktail or martini glass and garnish with the mint leaves.

Strawfruit

1 kiwifruit, peeled and coarsely chopped
3 fresh strawberries, hulled
Ice cubes
$1/_2$ oz (15 ml) apricot nectar
$1/_2$ oz (15 ml) cranberry juice
Soda water or lemonade, chilled

Place the kiwifruit and 2 strawberries in a glass and muddle until crushed. Fill the glass with some ice cubes and add the apricot nectar and cranberry juice. Top with the chilled soda water or lemonade and stir. Garnish with the remaining strawberry.

LEFT: Ginger and Peach Punch

Hot Drinks

Hot drinks are the great pretenders of the cocktail world.
They taste great and warm you up after a hard day.

Affogato

1 scoop vanilla ice cream
$1/_3$ cup (90 ml) hot espresso coffee
1 oz (30 ml) Kahlúa

Place the ice cream in a heatproof glass and pour the hot espresso coffee and kahlúa over the ice cream.

Corretto

$1/_4$ cup (60 ml) half-and-half
cream (half milk, half cream)
$1/_2$ oz (15 ml) amaretto
$1/_2$ cup (125 ml) hot strong
espresso coffee

1 Using a coffee machine steam wand, froth the half-and-half cream and amaretto until hot. Alternatively, heat the cream and amaretto in a small saucepan over low heat for about 1 minute, stirring constantly.
2 Pour the hot coffee into a heatproof glass and add the hot cream mixture. Serve immediately.

Mulled Wine

5 sugar cubes
4 cups (1 liter) red wine
2 cinnamon sticks
1 strip lemon zest
1 oz (30 ml) curaçao

Serves 4

1 In a nonreactive saucepan, combine the sugar cubes, wine, cinnamon sticks and lemon zest and cook over medium heat until a gray scum appears on the surface of the wine. Do not boil. Remove from the heat.
2 Skim the scum from the surface of the mixture and stir in the curaçao. Allow the drink to stand for about 5 minutes, then strain and serve warm.

Winter Warmer

1 teaspoon green tea leaves
1 cup (250 ml) boiling water
1 oz (30 ml) Scotch whisky
1 oz (30 ml) fresh lemon juice
1 tablespoon honey

1 Place the tea leaves in a teapot and pour the boiling water over. Cover and allow the mixture to steep.
2 Combine the Scotch, lemon juice and honey in a heatproof glass. Strain the tea and add to the glass, then stir and serve.

RIGHT: Affogato

Ingredient Glossary

absinthe: An anise-flavored liqueur that is illegal in the US because it is based on the wormwood plant. Pernod should be substituted where absinthe is unavailable.

Absolut Mandarin/Citron/Kurant: Flavored vodkas from the Absolut brand.

amaretto: A liqueur flavored with almonds, apricot kernels and seeds.

Angostura bitters: An aromatic mix of a variety of botanicals; the seeds, roots, leaves, fruit, bark and stems of various flora in an alcoholic base.

Aperol: An Italian aperitif similar to Campari and tasting of burnt oranges.

Bacardi: A well-known brand of rum with many varieties, including white rum and Bacardi 151 rum (see rum).

Baileys Irish Cream: A rich, sweet liqueur made with cream and Irish whiskey; Baileys was the first brand to make it.

Bénédictine: An aromatic herbal liqueur originally invented by a Benedictine monk in the sixteenth century.

berry-infused vodka: Vodka that has had berries soaking in it until the flavor imbues the spirit (see also Flavored spirits, page 15).

blue curaçao: An orange-flavored liqueur (see curaçao).

bourbon: A type of whiskey distilled from grains (mostly maize but also barley and rye) and aged in oak barrels, and available in various ages and blends.

brandy: A spirit made from distilling wine, fermented fruit juice or fruit pulp, brandy is also known as eau-de-vie; its quality usually depends on its age.

cachaça: A Brazilian rum distilled from sugarcane juice, cachaça has a sweet taste and a subtle rum flavor, with overtones of vanilla and various herbal flavors.

Calvados: A fine, powerful apple brandy made in France. Similar products include applejack from the US and apple brandy from England.

Campari: A popular Italian bitter aperitif with a brilliant red hue and strong quinine underpinnings.

Chambord: A raspberry-based liqueur made in France.

Champagne: The sparkling white wines produced from the Champagne region in France.

Chartreuse: A complex, aromatic liqueur which has been made by Carthusian monks near Grenoble, France, since 1605; it is available in both yellow and green versions.

Cherry Heering: A brand of rich, flavorsome cherry liqueur from Denmark.

chili-infused vodka: Vodka that has had chilies soaking in it until the flavor imparts the spirit (see Flavored spirits, page 15).

Cognac: A very fine brandy which is aged in special oak casks for 60 or 70 years.

crème de cacao: Chocolate-flavored liqueur, available in both white and dark.

crème de cassis: A black currant-flavored liqueur.

crème de framboise: A raspberry-flavored liqueur.

crème de mûre: A blackberry-flavored liqueur.

curaçao: An intense orange-flavored liqueur made from the peels of green oranges from the island of Curaçao. Available in clear orange and blue.

Dubonnet: A fortified wine from France.

eau-de-vie de fraise: Strawberry brandy; also called framboise.

eau-de-vie framboise sauvage: Wild raspberry brandy.

fraise des bois: A version of crème de fraise (liqueur) using wild strawberries.

framboise: see eau-de-vie de fraise.

Frangelico: An Italian hazelnut and herb liqueur.

fruit liqueurs: Flavored liqueurs (banana, quince, raspberry, ginger, cherry, strawberry, lychee, etc) which are sweet and mainly used as mixers in cocktails.

gin: A finely distilled spirit based on grains but characteristically flavored by additional blends of herbs and fruits; gin is not aged.

ginger juice: The liquid extracted from ginger when crushed or put through a juice extractor.

ginger syrup: A ginger-flavored syrup (see Syrups, page 15).

Jaggard Original: An Australian liqueur made from quandongs (a bush plum). Substitute plum juice, plum liqueur or slivovitz.

Kahlúa: A brand of sweet, rich coffee-flavored liqueur; originally from Mexico.

lemon verbena liqueur: A liqueur made from the lemon-scented leaves of lemon verbena.

Licor 43: A vanilla-flavored Spanish liqueur.

Lillet: A vermouth made with wine, fruit juice and herbs. Available white (Lillet Blanc) or red (Lillet Rouge).

lime cordial: A nonalcoholic syrup used as a mixer in drinks.

lychee juice: The juice from crushed and strained lychees.

Mandarin Napoleon: A type of curaçao, made with the skins of tangerines.

Monin Lime: A French liqueur flavored with limes.

Old Krupnik: A Polish honey liqueur.

orange bitters: A type of bitters with an orange base.

orgeat syrup: An almond-flavored syrup.

Pimms: An English liqueur flavored with fruit extracts.

pisco: A Latin American brandy.

prosecco: An Italian sparkling wine.

Poire William: A delicately flavored French pear eau-de-vie.

rum (dark, white and golden): one of the five main spirits, rum is made from sugarcane juice or molasses and comes in varying strengths and flavors. Notable brands include Bacardi, Captain Morgan, Havana Club and Mount Gay.

sake: A Japanese liquor produced from rice, commonly known as rice wine.

schnapps: Distilled, intensely flavored sweet liqueurs, schnapps is available in many varieties, from peach and apple to hazelnut or butterscotch.

Scotch whisky: Any of the whiskys made in Scotland.

slivovitz: A fruit brandy or eau-de-vie from Europe, made with black plums.

sloe gin: Gin flavored with the fruit of the wild blackthorn bush.

sour cherry syrup: A sweet, cherry-flavored nonalcoholic syrup.

tequila: A spirit distilled from the root of the blue agave plant and available in various types, including blanco (white) tequila, which is the original colorless version.

Triple Sec: An orange-flavored liqueur.

vodka: Originally distilled from potatoes but now more commonly made from grains, this highly refined spirit is colorless, odorless and flavorless; but flavored vodkas are also available (see Absolut).

Complete List of Recipes

Blended Cocktails
Banana and Pineapple
    Refresher 53
Banana Fizz 55
Berry Splice 50
Berry Surprise 56
Candy Pop 50
Caper and Chili Juice 53
Coconut Holiday 59
Fruit Daiquiris 56
Golden Banana 55
Grand Mango 49
Honeydew and Kiwifruit
    Daiquiri 53
Pear Diaquiri 59
Sgroppino 55
Slivovitz Plum Daiquiri 50

Built Cocktails
Blackberry Emergency 62
Citrus Fountain 79
Cranberry Apple Sour 76
Ginger and Mandarin Sea
    Breeze 75
Ginger Melon 71
Ginger "n" Orange 72
Gingerene 76
Guava Vogue 79
King 75
Lifesaver 75
Napoleon 79
Pisco Sour 71
Soda and Citrus 71
Soda Nut 72
Sunshine 75
Tiberian Sun 72
Wild Strawberries 76

Champagne Cocktails
Adam's Apple 38
Alasia 37
Croatian Cherry 38
French 75 34
One-five-one 38

Peach Bubbles 37

Classic Cocktails
Bellini 23
Bloody Mary 17
Brandy Alexander 32
Caipirinha 24
Cosmopolitan 28
Daiquiri 31
Gimlet 23
Grasshopper 27
James Bond 20
Kir Royale 23
Long Island Iced Tea 18
Mai Tai 32
Manhattan 20
Margarita 24
Mint Julep 28
Mojito 31
Moscow Mule 20
Pina Colada 24
Rob Roy 28
Sea Breeze 27
Singapore Sling 18
Tom Collins 28

Crushed Cocktails
Apple Man 62
Berry Caipiroska 65
Blood Orange Crush 62
Caiperol 62
Caipiroska 65
Eau de Coing 66
Gin Club 66
Ginger Mojito 66
Grapefruit Caipiroska 65
Jaggard Crush 66
Passion Fruit Caipiroska 60
Pine Lime Crush 65
Tangerine Cooler 62

Hot Drinks
Affogato 92
Corretto 92

Mulled Wine 92
Winter Warmer 92

Martinis
Apple Martini 42
Audience Martini 45
Beetle 46
Berry Martini 45
Crown Martini 42
Hazelnut Martini 42
Honey Martini 45
Killer Martini 40
Lemon Warhead 46
Rose Water Cinnamon
    Martini 42
Sake Martini 46
Scud Martini 40
Strange Keys 46
Vanilla Martini 45
Watermelon Martini 46

Nonalcoholic Cocktails
Crenshaw 89
Ginger Peach Punch 91
Strawfruit 91
Tropicana 91
Tutti Frutti 89

Shaken and Strained Cocktails
Blanc 86
Blood Berries 85
Cherry Tree 81
Green Fairy 82
Margarita No.5 82
Peach Apricot Shaker 85
Pimms Green Tea Refresher 86
Raspberry Collins 82
Raspberry Sourgear 82
Sour Morning 86
Spitfire 85
Strawberry Hills 85
Tangerine Sour 81
Verbs 86